I0162756

JuárOz

A Poetic Fiction

Ger Killeen

Headlandia Press, Portland, Oregon

Cállate. Nadie sabe que estás en mí,
toda entera. Cállate. No respires. Nadie
sabe mi merienda suculenta de unidad:
légion de oscuridades, amazonas de lloro.

Shush. No one knows that you are in me,
every single one of you. Shush. Don't breathe. No one
knows my succulent picnic of unity:
legion of obscurities, amazons of weeping.

(César Vallejo, *Trilce, LXXI*)

Contents

Fellow travelers

Fellow revelers, I met their lanky columns on the retreat from 'La Tercera Cara' after the cyan hours prised away the objects from the actions. Not a trace anywhere in the alleys of pity or fear, just the starry shimmer of voided liquids. We had come to this with our lusty cameras, to soak an unending carnival in the acids of our sociological distain. I could already see myself later in an El Paso fern bar confiding *my dead friend, Pedro* and *there was a girl, Ramona*, phrases I could draw across myself as though actual scars had marked my passage. Say I was there. Say you were there.

We can make this scenario up on the model of a porn film which is the deep structure of all norteño narratives, the maw that devours the motherly pie. Scene One, Interior: They buy the girls drinks. Scene Two, Exterior: They all get into a black Chevy Suburban. Scene Three, Exterior: Penetration, Death. The moment of revelation where nothing is left, sunlight filing away consciousness and conscience in the never-ending morning of platitudes. Is this news to you?

That's the stuff. On the other side, they lap it up with us.

Antique Land

(He) passes wall after wall: a retablo of Santa Barbara, a retablo of Santa Elena de la Cruz, a retablo of San Luis Gongzaga, a retablo of La Puirisma Concepcion, a retablo of San Andres Avelino, a retablo of San Camilo de Lelis, a retablo of El Niño Cautivo, a retablo of El Niño de Atocha, a retablo of Ojo de Díos, a retablo of San Pascual Bailon, a retablo of El Sueño de Jesús, a retablo of El Señor de las Peñas, a retablo of San Ysidro Labrador, a retablo of Anima Sola, a retablo of Nuestra Señora de Carmen, a retablo of La Sagrada Familia, a retablo of San Expedito, a retablo of Santa Eduviges, a retablo of La Preciosa Sangre.

Then a whole room of sabino tables, chestnut credenzas, rosewood caskets, camphor-wood cofres, fruitwood desks, walnut roperos, and cedar bargueños.

In a glass case crammed with relics (he) finds a small silver box with a human tooth in the embrace of its dusty, red velvet lining. Another man would have haggled. Not (he). "It spoke to (me)", (he) says. "Literally":

I am the left maxillary cuspid of Jesús Malverde. Place me under your pillow at night and you will dream the maps of the safest routes; you will see those you can trust and those you cannot; you will escape before the raids happen; you will find wealth; you will find love. In return you must follow my instructions and be kind to the poor.

"And after that", (he) says, "(he) never looked back."

Trunkless, Vast

Like wind, like bees.
Me gustaría que.
Lift a stone, nothing there.
Their names drift in the dune fields,
last rasps of understanding
that catch on the graythorn
with the bleached shreds of plastic.

The yellowy trails ramify
in the irises of the detectives
who can no longer connect anything with anything with
anything.
Las lágrimas.
Lift a tire, nothing there.
The detectives try to lean on
the bitten hours *de aquellos que sufren.*
Lift a fingernail, nothing there.
Like bees, like wind,
the sublime border
between language and the noise
that is the vascular system of silence.

Sequen ante el sol.
Like wind, like bees,
like lifting your hands
against the deluge
of another night's sequent unworking
of connections.
Someone remembers

someone hearing
about someone
seeing something
that turns out to be nothing.
Lift a veil, nothing there.
El día haya terminado.

Dries off. Dries out. Dries up.

Legs

A teetering, tawny glint at the edge of the dancefloor—
such glory was it to (him), the country between the
miniskirt's hem and the ruby stiletto's open toed end,
figure detatched from agency, come-on-in-itself, final
answer to unformulated prayer, excavatable treasure
among the rubble of shes.

These same various ones, her and her and her,
detatched and scratched with the clumsy x's of a
primitive yet undeciphered script, posed with care to
form a solar cross on the traffic island between
Avenida___ and Calle___, are the culmination of the
long ex voto tradition of those who have miraculously
come through.

(His) offering magnifies (him) and (him) and (him)
through (his) public anonymity. (He) plays their screams
on (his) iPod in the car alone, cruising these night rivers
out of paradise.

Standing In the Desert

She tells me her first real boyfriend had a detailed map of Sonora tattooed on his back and a map of Chihuahua on his front. Once he said to her that she should get a map of New Mexico tattooed on her stomach and Texas on her ass so that he could always be fucking Gringoland. He was crazy angry with the USA. The Migra caught him fifty times before he stopped trying to cross over but he claimed it was good training for his career because it made him tough and filled him with hate. *Hate is an energy, baby, and the heart is a battery where you can store it until you need it. Then, boom, look out!* The week after he died in a shootout with the Federal police she decided to have a streetmap of the area where he was killed tattooed on her chest. She takes off her t-shirt and bra and rubs her left nipple until it's purplehard. *There's where they shot him down.* She takes my finger and puts it on her navel. *And this is about where we're standing now.*

Shattered Visage

Near   the Guernika   hospital
   families are   thrusting
photo   copied   flyers into
the open   mouth

of November. First
             Communion photos,
  Confirmation   photos,
    Quinceañera portraits
               dance in the streets.
Outside   school   the sleek menboys
are conjugating the verb "kill":
I eat, she falls, we fuck, you die.

The posters   drain
  away   from the lamposts,
  eyes melt,   skin melts,
       hair melts,   print melts,
  a gray sap
  invading
       the inexhaustible
            devotions
of dreamwork, carving
        rivulets
between

the glabella   *the supraorbital process*

through

the masticated names
sofíavalentinaisabellacamilagabrielaximena

down to the cryless desert sea.

Lip

She was about twelve
when she got the best
advice on TV: to first use a red-
orange pencil, line them
before applying a light
red gloss, something good,
expensive looking,
like E.L.F.'s *Labial Líquido Seductor.*
Cost a fortune.
If she'd won the Miss Maquila
competition
she'd have been made
for life.
   But...you know how it goes.
She tells me my Spanish is so awful
that when I speak
she can hardly tell if I'm saying
maquilar, "to assemble"
or *maquillar* "to put on makeup",
that if I wanted
she could give me lessons,
$10 for an hour, OK, for two hours.

Never saw her again.

Sneer

Here she is.
She's looking the worse for wear,
but her voice is surprisingly strong.
A little hoarse, maybe, but strong.
She's sitting on the dirt floor,
her arms tied above her
to the bars on the small cellar window behind her,
a tall, skinny woman
bruises all over her face,
covered in grime from head to lovely foot,
with matted long black hair,
wearing nothing;
her once-white blouse and sparkly blue skirt
are tossed over in a corner. She should be the picture
of pure victimhood
but as she tries to focus her eyes
and keep her head upright
she gives off a kind of nobility.
(I)'ve seen that in a few others
over the years
and normally it infuriates (me)
and (I) make them pay.
But with her...it does nothing but intrigue (me).
She'll pay later.
(I)'m sitting in an uncomfortable pink plastic deck-chair,
looking at her.
(I)'m aware

that (I)'m tapping (my) pistol against (my) thigh.
She's trying to make (me) out
through the pain and the dim light.
Is that you, Teo? Teodoro, is that you? Teo?
(I)'m not going to answer.
I know it's you, Teo. Just tell me it's you, will you, Teo? I
don't want anything,   Teo, I just want to hear a voice
before...Tell me it's you there Teo.
It's me, (I) lie. Some ex-boyfriend maybe.
Good. Thank you, Teo, she says,
and (I) have a sense that she really means it,
that she's glad,
somehow (I)'ve given her something
that makes all the difference.
She falls
silent, her head
propped back against the wall
and there's almost a look of contentment
showing through the flesh of her swollen face.
(I) wonder if she might be going
to pass out or maybe die.
No she can't be going to die, she's not even close.
In the gray silence (I) hear her
breathing through her mouth,
and (I) hear (my) own regular, sluggish heartbeat inside
(my) head.
Strangely, (I) want her to say more, but she doesn't.
There's a sudden burst of music
from the corner where her clothes are thrown.
Her cell phone goes off loudly

with 'Mi Piquito de Oro' by Ramon Ayala.
It startles (us (both.
(I) am also surprised at her choice of ringtone.
(I) would have thought she'd have something more
restrained, a woman like her.
(I) fish it out from under the clothes
and see the name LauraB come up on the screen.
Who is it, Teo?, she says without moving her head.
Laura, (I) say, *Laura B*. The ringtone keeps playing.
She's waiting for me at the restaurant.
I'm never late, you know.
The music stops.
After a few seconds there's a little ping.
A text appears.
'Girl where r u Call me'.
(I) take the phone and open the camera.
(I) walk over to her, move her thighs
farther apart with (my) boot.
Then (I) step back and snap a pic.
The flash goes off like lightning.
Then (I) send it to Laura
with the message 'You're next cunt'.
(I) switch off the phone and toss it away.
In (my) head (I) see
the explosion of horror and terror
at a good table in a good restaurant
with waiters and waitresses in neat uniforms
buzzing around.
It feels like the first sip
of a bottle of chilled beer

on a warm day.
(I) can't suppress a smile.

Sculptor

Everything here speaks
submission, Ramona tells me,
a relinquishment of power more
or less voluntary now
that the downcast look
and the shiteating smile
have been passed down
through uncountable generations.
There was a Chilean sculptor
who excavated
the word SUMISION
right there, in the shadow
of Black Christ Mountain
beside the shacks,
practically on the border,
practically in
the dumping ground for bodies,
in letters 15 meters high;
the idea was to fill
each letter trench with fuel
and set it on fire so that the word would flame up
for 30 minutes and be filmed from a plane.
They dug out the word
in huge Helvetica font letters
(personally, I'd have chosen Perpetua,
she sniggers), but before
they could set it aflame
they were stopped by the cops.

A few days later, she says, I went
and had SUMISIÓN
tattooed just above my pubic hairline
in letters entwined in flames and desert roses
which the tattoo artists
around here
are especially good at.
It freaked my husband out.
Beginning of the end
for *that* marriage.

Those Passions

I'll sing you this corrido of The Scorpion of the Night
Who was feared by cops and scum throughout
Chihuahua,
Who was born as poor as Jesus, but man, could that kid
fight!
And he fought his way to wealth and fame and honor.

At fourteen he took his chance and took out a stinking
snitch,
And the cartel said "Good boy, you're one of us now",
And NO job was too big, he made everyone his bitch,
With an AK, safety off, and good to go, good to go.

He lived off three animals, didn't need to buy them
food.
They brought him cash, he loved them as life itself;
Ah what animals! His parakeet, his rooster, his nanny
goat,
They traveled with him from the mountains to the Gulf.

Now the Scorpion loved young women as all the real
men do,
Not a virgin north of Hidalgo but he didn't capture,
And until he met Lucinda every night was someone
new,
But with Lucy he was introduced to rapture.

Every man will swear on his mother there was *llello* in
her gaze,
That her swinging hips would make you come just

looking,
And the night the Scorpion met her he fell into a daze,
And he fell under those stars that are unlucky.

Ah, boys, we know it well, to fall under a woman's spell
Makes you careless, makes you tender, makes you
weak.
Your enemies have their spies and your soft spots they
can tell
And they'll bide their time until they make their strike.

So while he slept in Lucy's arms, a Sinaloa gang
Broke through his door with automatics blazing.
They shot them both to shreds, cut off the Scorpion's
head,
And spiked it on the bridge in front of Juárez.

So, listen well, my friends, and don't meet the
Scorpion's end,
Don't ever let lovely lips and tits ensnare you.
Keep your AK as your bride, keep your secrets in the
sand,
Be certain no one loves you more than fears you.

These Lifeless Things

"The remains"
"of an unidentified"
"woman, between the ages of 15 and 20",
"were come upon"
"in a trench near"
"an unauthorized"
"garbage dump"
"the body",
"wrapped in a bedsheet"
"and stuffed inside a large plastic bag",
"showed signs of extreme violence".
"She was wounded",
"presumably by a dagger",
"in the back, chest, genitals, and neck".
"Authorities"
"have established"
"that the woman was murdered"
"in a different place"
"and was then dumped"
"where she was found".
"Authorities"
"are still unsure"
"if she was sexually assaulted".

Nota Bene: advanced decomposition
can result in skin lesions
that mimic stab wounds.
In reality,
the skin is breaking down

due to the decomposition process.
It is vital
in such cases to evaluate
carefully
the tissues underlying the skin,
to distinguish true
sharp force injuries
from decomposition.
However, the tissues of victims
of sharp force injury can certainly
decompose. In such settings,
the true
injuries can become altered
by the decomposition
itself.

Mock

My hands have never been the same, she says.
Every day, twelve hour shift, sometimes overtime,
thousands and thousands of rag dolls with the plastic
head of a princess from some Disney movie. I had to
dress the dolls as they went by on a conveyor belt,
really really fast. I had to pull their gauzy pink dresses
on from the neck down, fasten three tiny buttons, and
off they went to have a crown glued on their heads.
Over and over and over. If you stopped even for a
minute, dolls would start to pile up and everyone would
get mad. Not just the asshole supervisor but the other
girls because our team got a production bonus if we
exceeded a certain number. I lasted nine months.
 My cousin though, that's the saddest story. She worked
at a place that made satellite dishes where she soldered
small parts together. She was beautiful and her
supervisor kept hitting on her, but she had a boyfriend
so she kept saying no. Her team decided that she should
be the one who would enter the Miss Maquila beauty
contest and at home I'd help her practice the correct
walk, the way to swing her hips. A few days before the
pageant something blew up at her work station and
splashed muriatic acid into her face. They rushed her to
the showers but it was too late—her skin was ruined.
There was a rumor the supervisor did it. They gave her
some money but told her she couldn't work there
anymore, that's what they do.
 She started working with me at the doll factory but she

24

became more and more depressed. Her fucking boyfriend took off. She wouldn't go out to clubs any more. She was the slowest worker on the line, always getting written up.

One night she didn't come home after the end of the shift. I looked everywhere for her, hospitals, morgue, even police stations. Not a trace. For weeks I called people back in Durango to see if she'd run back there. Not a sign of her. Her mother used to phone me up and scream at me saying it was my fault she was missing because I lured her north to be a filthy whore like me. She said worse things.

That was five years ago. I have a picture of her before the acid that I used to put up around the town until some woman said that was stupid since now she looked like a creature from a movie and no one would recognize her. I beat the shit out of that woman. But, you know, she was right.

Heart That Fed

Midnight is the loveliest hour, disgorging
fresh girls out of the assembly plants, mixing
money with desire, churning
the world up
into the lilac froth of a sodium-lit fantasia.
(He) can gaze through her
flesh to the heart, *this one*,crawl
after the transport bus
in (his) SUV, wait, wait, wait
until she a-
lights to walk the lightless
alleys
home

When (he) reclines (he) is
the bowl catching
the decay of her heart's
harmonics over the hours. (He) sings
the dripping syllables
of (his) own novena hymn
to Santisima Muerte,
just as (his) father before (him) sang
and (his) father's father, all
the way back
to the first gods,
the first gods' hunger.

On A Pedestal

She is aplomb in the whorl of (his) ear
and her tongue is in (his) tongue
and her nipple is (his) scapular
she has the color of (his) cum
she is engulfed in (his) sleep
like a fossil in the sand.

Her thighs are always open
and will not let him wake
her rattles in broad daylight
make roses of (his) hate
make (him) sing and shout and sing
cry "mama" and "mija"
when there's nothing else to say.

Names

While we sleep the phonemes sift inside us from the dunefields. These ones fly all the way back to Zinacantán, the capital of new urgency, where the old women decode dreams in real time. Night after night, girl after girl, this one in shreds of her school uniform, that one in scraps of her maquila smock, mouth the missing pieces of the world. One throws at us her severed nipple attached to the end of a fishing line. "Ido", she whispers, and draws it back. Then another does the same. Then another. Over and over. At the point of revelation their lips blur, eyes become smoke. The killers reach that far, and farther. Strife of tongue, confusion of flesh, we assist at a great feast of branding, you and I. Whole villages are going mad, knowing and not knowing.

My Works

automotive prototype design automotive seat covers
computer assembly signal cables telecommunications
cocaine transporation cardiovascular medical
equipment dead women printer cartridges bootleg dvds
refrigerators dryers landscape products fabrication
dead men automotive electronic boards circuit boards
whores washing machines plastic toys marijuana
transportation computer assembly dead women
computer assembly dead women computer assembly
automatic weapons disposable surgery equipment
television sets dolls narcocorridos paint industrial
chemicals cleaning products photocopiers pink crosses
mobile phones

Round the Decay

Lupita tells me the dump was its own world. You knew there was another world beyond it, but that other world was even more frightening to you. The dump was home. The area she lived in was called Sangre de Cristo. The story was that years before there had been a bad war between two rival gangs for control of this part of the dump. People were getting killed daily, including kids. Everyone was terrified, but no one could make it stop. Priests would come in, Christian missionaries, all trying to arrange a truce, but nothing worked. Even some of the peacemakers were killed.

Well, after one especially bad night of killings a huge crowd of dump-people had gathered on top of a high garbage hill to pray. Yeah, there was wailing and crying and chanting, and down below members of one of the gangs were hanging around laughing. Suddenly someone noticed a movement about half way down the hill. Out of the ground was coming a small fountain of red colored liquid. In minutes it got bigger and burst out in a torrent and flowed down to where the gang members were standing. People on the top of the hill said they felt an earthquake as the liquid was gushing out. The gangsters just stood there as the liquid flowed down to where they were and sloshed around them. That's when the miracle happened: they tried to run off but they couldn't. They started stumbling around and then dropping like flies, coughing and choking. Someone on the hill started shouting "The blood of

Christ defeats you!" and before long everyone was shouting the same thing, as the gangsters fell down and died. They say eight of them died and five were turned into living corpses who didn't last long afterwards. Anyway, it was a miracle and it put an end to the war. Ever since then the whole western area of the dump has been called Sangre de Cristo. That's where she lived. Every year there's a memorial procession to the top of that hill.

And everyone at the dump who was there that day says the red stuff was really blood. The old people all stuck to that story and passed it on to us, with trembling, with fear. A few even had little bottles of the stuff and they'd bring them out and make the sign of the cross with it on sick people or pregnant women or couples getting married.

You see, she says, when Jesus became a man he sanctified everything—even the canals of shit, the cascades of piss, the rolling hills of rot. And sometimes when things get really bad the sanctified flesh of the world bleeds for us. To remind us that God is suffering , suffering with us, the garbage people. The red stuff: we all swear by it. Amen, Lupita says, amen.

Colossal

My friend Pedro is murdered,
his body welded by flames
to a hollow among the dunes.
At the sunrise, sand-washed

gates we're puking bottled light
-ning in his memory, untoast-
    ing the border guards glass-
    ing us from the airy bridge of fate.

Northwards, like a puppet, stumbl
-ing, I fling my arms out, shout, *all of it,*
all this is mine, all of it,
while my friends howl and howl.

The Zetas say the Lineas did it.
The Lineas say the Police did it.

Bare the lone

Issues from the guard-towers
the times'
demotic light; it has come to this,
come back to this. In the late
Pleistocene catalog of power
tools the various scaly rimes
of terror look as remarkably uniform
as what accomplishes
the job of burring them off.
The labels are different
as barcodes,
a clever pricing
mechanism. When you get right down to it.
Down to it.

What you see, though, through:
into the tunnels angels descending
and descending, the slash of sirens
from which the canny flee like ants,
the whole desert one vast
graveyard of strobelit yearning.

Issue from the naked ground
the colossal plants,
the endless armies of the native insects
bathed in clouds of golden pheromones,
nights of scarlet teeth and ruby claws.
Everything waits.

In wait.
If you're by yourself,
you don't breathe a word.

Far Away

Some morning we'll wake up
and it will all be over she says.We'll look
at each other with our bald eyes
and we'll be pierced by the elemental luster
the sheen on each other's new faces.
I wonder if then we can know to weep.
I wonder if we'll be able
to bear the sight of each other
all shiny and shimmery and metallic
as the pigeons from the Córdova bridge
all of us become the names
of our sunscraped bones. I see
this future, a procession of zeros,
as though the empty ominous days at the end
of the previous calendar had swelled
and sent tendrils through the fat hours of living
sucking them dry even of ordinary griefs. Amen, then:
No news no time no sightings
no picture no progress no evidence
no crime no suspects no meetings
no time not here not available
not there not relevant not home,
not (his) case no resources no leads
no time no file no report
no log no call no body
no no no no no

About The Author

Ger Killeen is the author of several books of poetry including Lia A Léimfidh Thar Tonnta: A Stone That Will Leap Over The Waves *(Trask House, 1999),* A Wren *(Bluestem Press, winner of the Bluestem Award for Poetry),* Signs Following *(Parlor Press, 2005), and* Blood Orbits *(Parlor Press 2009)*

His work also appears in several anthologies including From Here We Speak *(Oregon State University Press),* American Poetry: The Next Generation *(Carnegie-Mellon University Press), and* The Gertrude Stein Awards *(Green Integer).*

He is the poetry editor at Elohi Gadugi Journal, *and at* The Habit of Rainy Nights Press. *He teaches at Marylhurst University near Portland, Oregon.*

He blogs at headlandia.blogspot.com

© Ger Killeen, 2014
All Rights Reserved

Headlandia Press, Portland, Oregon

www.ingramcontent.com/pod-product-compliance
Lightning Source LLC
Chambersburg PA
CBHW022349040426
42449CB00006B/788